616.9
MET   Metos, H. Thomas
        Communicable, Diseases
                        B.C.# 373

DATE DUE		
APR 30		
MAY 24		
MAY 1 8 1994		
MAR 0 7 1997		

Communicable Diseases

Thomas H. Metos

COMMUNICABLE DISEASES

616.9
MET

FRANKLIN WATTS
NEW YORK|LONDON|TORONTO|SYDNEY|1987
A FIRST BOOK

Photographs courtesy of: Centers for Disease Control: pp. 12, 13, 52, 55, 67 (Dr. Thomas Hooten), 80; Photo Researchers, Inc.: pp. 24 (top left— Dr. Tony Brain/Science Photo Library; top right—Ed Lettau; bottom— Donald Wong), 29 (Christopher Morrow), 38 (Ray Ellis), 46 (Larry Mulvehill), 51 (Lowell Georgia/Science Source); The Bettmann Archive, Inc.: pp. 32, 62; Taurus Photos: p. 41 (G. Anderson); WHO Photo: p. 75 (R. Phillips).

Library of Congress Cataloging-in-Publication Data

Metos, Thomas H.
Communicable diseases.

(A First book)
Bibliography: p.
Includes index.
Summary: Discusses the causes, diagnosis, and
classification of some diseases that are passed
from one human to another, including plagues,
sexually transmitted diseases, and the common cold.
1. Communicable diseases—Juvenile literature.
[1. Communicable diseases. 2. Diseases] I. Title.
RC111.M46 1987   616.9   87-8138
ISBN 0-531-10380-3

Contents

Communicable Diseases

Introduction

Have you ever thought of greasing your neck and chest with hot skunk oil the next time you catch a cold and sore throat, or of placing a dried rat's tail in a dirty sock and wrapping it around your sore throat to cure it? These are just two examples of folk medicine that many people even today believe can cure all sorts of diseases.

Many of the folk cures for disease are cures for communicable diseases, that is diseases that can be passed from one human to another, while other folk cures describe ways of curing birth deformities, wounds and cuts, and disease caused by other means than being transmitted from one person to another.

You may have heard someone say that one ought to feed a cold and starve a fever or that an apple a day keeps the doctor away. The cures for the disease, then, are to come from eating or not eating. Many people once believed that eating precious stones or metals (diamonds, pearls, rubies, gold, and silver) or rubbing the body with them would cure disease. Often only kings or queens could afford these remedies—they were just too expensive. The diamonds, pearls, rubies, or gold would be ground up into fine powder and mixed into wine, and drunk. Sometimes gold was dissolved using different chemicals, and drunk, injected, or applied to the body to cure wounds and diseases. Gold at one time was thought to be a cure for insanity and other mental illnesses.

Occasionally, though, scientists discover that certain medical folklore is true. For example, one longtime, widely used cure for a cold has been to eat lots of hot chicken soup. Recently, scientists have found that hot chicken soup will not cure a cold, but that the hot steam from the soup does help to clear your nose and makes a sore throat better.

Today we know a great deal more about diseases and how they are contracted. We know that some diseases are inherited, whereas some are the result of drug abuse or a nutritional imbalance. Sometimes a polluted environment is the culprit, and sometimes disease is caused by a variety of factors. Some diseases are passed from person to person—like the common cold or AIDS. These are among the communicable diseases, the subject of this book.

Chapter One

CAUSES OF COMMUNICABLE DISEASES

The major causes of human communicable diseases are (1) bacteria, (2) viruses, (3) fungi, (4) rickettsiae, and (5) parasites. Today these organisms are found throughout the world, and evidence of their existence has been found in prehistoric fossils and rock formations that are up to 395 million years old. Even ancient Egyptian mummies have shown evidence of diseases caused by viruses and bacteria.

In 1954, a naturally mummified body of a young Inca boy was found in his tomb by treasure hunters. The boy had been a sacrifice to the Inca god of the sun. Because he was buried in a very dry and frozen environment, his body, over five hundred years old, was perfectly preserved. Scientists, when examining the body, found some sores on the skin of the boy's hand. When the scientists examined samples of the sores under an electron microscope, they discovered that the viruses that caused the sores could still be seen. They were so small that two hundred thousand or more could fit on the end of a pencil.

Bacteria are also very small one-cell organisms. They are found almost everywhere in the world, and without them life as we know it could not exist. That is because the majority of bacteria are not harmful to people and many are necessary for plant growth and

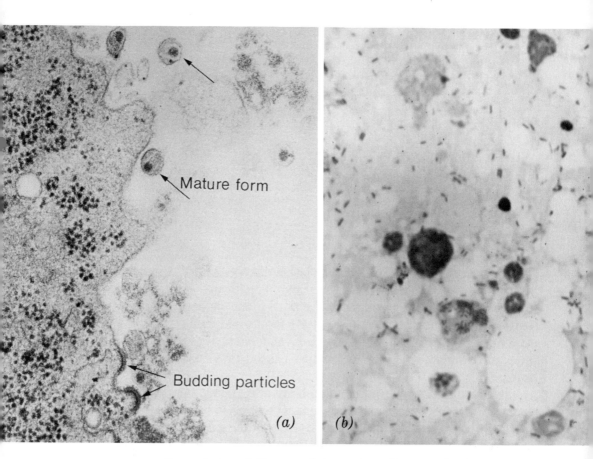

Mature form

Budding particles

(a)   (b)

Organisms of disease: (a) a microphotograph of the
HTLV-III/LAV virus, the cause of AIDS, the most frightening
communicable disease of modern times; (b) rickettsiae,
shown here under a microscope as dark stains, are the cause
of Rocky Mountain spotted fever and typhus; (c) a child
with impetigo, a contagious skin disease caused by bacteria;
(d) ringworm, a fungus-caused disease, easily transmitted from
person to person; and (e) a tunnel in the skin produced by the
infective-stage larvae of a hookworm, a parasite

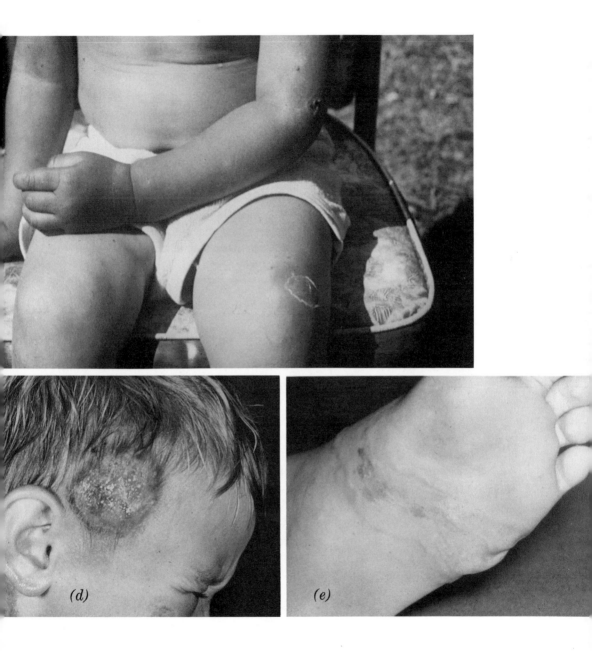

(d)

(e)

the processing of food. The next time you eat a piece of cheese, remember that cheese could not be made without bacteria.

Bacteria can be active at temperatures from around 32°F (0°C) up to 160°F (71°C). When conditions are right, they can grow very rapidly and multiply every fifteen minutes. Humans always have bacteria living and growing in and on them—in the mouth and intestinal tract and on the skin. Most of the time these bacteria do not cause problems. However, at times the bacteria's growth is not controlled by the body, and that is when an infection or disease may occur.

Some bacteria will cause only specific diseases in certain parts of the body. For example, certain bacteria will attack the brain and cause meningitis; others will attack the throat and cause diphtheria. One group, the staphylococcal bacteria, will attack the body almost anywhere.

Viruses are very small organisms. They are so small that they cannot be seen by using a regular, or light, microscope. Only an electron microscope, which can magnify objects much more than a light microscope, makes viruses visible.

Because viruses are such small and simple organisms, some scientists believe that they are neither living nor nonliving matter and classify them somewhere between. Viruses consist only of a genetic material and a covering. They become "alive" only when they invade a cell and start to reproduce and multiply. Some scientists once believed that viruses were a link between nonliving substance and living cells. Some scientists today believe that viruses have evolved from bacteria.

There are many kinds of viruses that cause disease in humans. These range from viruses that cause eye inflammation and the flu to viruses that cause serious diseases such as polio and rubella (German measles). There seems to be growing evidence that some viruses appear to be related to some noninfectious diseases such as cancer and diabetes.

So-called slow viruses invade the body but do not cause a disease until many years later. A person may be infected at the age of forty by the virus, but it may be years before the disease affects the body. Most of these slow viruses cause degenerative diseases, a decline in a person's physical abilities. If the virus attacks the brain, the disease almost always ends in death.

Rickettsiae-caused diseases are not commonly found in the United States. *Rickettsiae* are small bacterialike organisms that cause such diseases as Rocky Mountain spotted fever, Q fever, and typhus. These are life-threatening diseases that are transmitted to humans by way of insects.

Fungi, like bacteria and viruses, are found everywhere in the world. However, like most bacteria, fungi need oxygen in order to grow. Fungi show great variety in size and complexity. They range from microscopic one-celled organisms to very large and complicated organisms like puffballs.

Fungi can be both helpful and harmful to humans. Fungi are helpful because they cause animal and plant materials to decay, returning needed chemicals to the soil and in the process removing wastes. Also, some mushrooms, which are fungi, are good to eat. (But some types of mushrooms are harmful, because they are poisonous when eaten.) Yeast is a fungus which is necessary to make beer and most breads. Some antibiotic drugs, like penicillin, are made from fungus, or mold, as are some cheeses.

Yet, some fungi can cause disease in humans. The most common fungal infections which can be passed from one person to another are those that affect the skin, hair, or fingernails. These are commonly called athlete's foot, barber's itch, and ringworm. These diseases can be easily transmitted from person to person.

Ringworm is a fungus-caused disease that may affect various parts of the body. When it affects the feet, we call it athlete's foot; when it attacks the crotch we call it jock itch. The disease can become *endemic*, or localized, when it breaks out in a school or army barracks, or among those people who use a gym or a swimming pool. It is either passed directly from person to person or transmitted through contact with contaminated shoes, towels, or shower stalls.

Ringworm causes small raised spots on the skin that may be dry and scaly or moist and crusty. The disease gets its name because as the spots enlarge, the centers heal and the spots become ring-shaped.

The disease is easily diagnosed by a doctor because of the ring-shaped spots. However, in its early stages, skin scrapings can be examined under a microscope to confirm the diagnosis.

Fortunately, the various types of ringworm can usually be eliminated by use of the drug griseofulvin or antifungal powders. In cases when secondary bacterial infection occurs, antibiotic drugs will also have to be given.

There are other fungi that can cause diseases much more serious than ringworm—diseases that can be fatal if not treated, such as Valley fever. Most of these diseases are ordinarily not communicated from one person to another. The infection is caused when the fungus is breathed in or invades the bloodstream by way of a cut or abrasion.

Parasitic diseases are caused by over fifty different protozoa and helminths. Protozoa are the simplest single-celled animals. Rather than cell walls, they have cell membranes and their centers are surrounded by membranes. Helminths are worms.

Many parasitic diseases can be very serious, like malaria and sleeping sickness, and are often found in the tropical areas of the world. These diseases are transmitted to humans by insects. Other protozoan-caused diseases are spread to humans by contact with water or food contaminated with human feces.

Helminth-, or worm-, caused diseases are transmitted usually by people eating infected food, contact with infected soil or water, and, occasionally, by direct human contact. The worms, after entering the human, will then locate in various parts of the body to gain nourishment and multiply. For example, hookworms will locate and stay in the intestinal tract, some round worms will finally locate in muscles, while others will migrate to the lungs and other organs to live out their lives.

Chapter Two

CLASSIFICATION
OF DISEASES

It is very important that scientists, doctors, and governments know about kinds, types, and numbers of diseases that occur in a nation, state, or city. For example, it is important to know whether the cases of certain communicable diseases, such as measles or chicken pox, are increasing or decreasing. If they are increasing, the health officials will know that people are not being immunized and that an immunization program needs to be started or that TV or newspaper ads need to inform people that immunization is needed. That is why governments keep statistics about diseases and especially the causes of deaths in humans.

Also, statistics about causes of death sometimes reveal a high incidence of a certain disease among certain groups of people, and this information may allow scientists to discover the cause of the disease. For example, in this way scientists were able to discover that people who smoked cigarettes had a much higher rate of lung cancer than nonsmokers and then established that one of the major causes of lung cancer was smoking.

Though there are a number of different ways to classify diseases, one of the most widely used systems is by the way that

How diseases are transmitted

Contact

Common vehicle

Airborne

Vector-borne

diseases are transmitted. The four ways that diseases are transmitted are by contact, common vehicle, air, and vector.

Contact diseases are transmitted directly from person to person by means of such objects as contaminated drinking glasses. *Common vehicle* refers most often to food or water that is contaminated with disease-carrying organisms. *Airborne* refers to transmission of infectious agents through the air. *Vector-borne* diseases are transmitted by insects.

There are a number of other ways that diseases can be classified. For example, sometimes diseases are referred to as diseases of old age, children's diseases, viral or bacterial diseases, or sexual diseases. Other classifications often used refer to the severity of the disease or to the affected organ.

Chapter Three

DEFENSE MECHANISMS

Homeostasis is a word used to describe the process the body uses to regulate itself to maintain good health. The tissues and the organs of the body, then, constantly act together to maintain the internal environment of the body within very narrow limits.

For example, the human body must keep its temperature fairly close to 98.6°F (37°C). If the body temperature exceeds 98.6°F, it may mean that we have a disease. But humans are constantly moving from one temperature environment to another—for example, in December you may go from your house, which is heated to 75°F (24°C), to outside where the temperature is well below freezing. In order for the inner core of the body to maintain its temperature and homeostasis, some of the blood from your hands, feet, and face is drawn into the inner core. So, when you are out in a snowstorm, your body lets your hands and feet get cold to keep your heart, lungs, liver, and other organs warm. When you go from an air-conditioned room to play outside in July, when the temperature may be close to 100°F (38°C), your body then causes your skin to sweat in order to keep the internal body temperature constant.

The body uses a number of devices to maintain homeostasis. Among these are reflexes. For example, if you touch a very hot object, such as a stove top, your hand is automatically pulled away by the reflex action. Other ways the body communicates with itself is through the use of various chemicals, such as calcium, in the cells and tissues. Calcium keeps the body homeostatic (in homeostasis) by moving into and out of cells and telling them how to react. Calcium has an important use in telling the muscles of the body when to contract or relax.

Homeostasis, then, is very important in maintaining an individual's health. For if the body's temperature, fluids, and chemical balance, and the process of using food to create energy become out of balance, the result could be illness or even death. One way that a person can help the homeostatic process in the body is to have good health habits. A healthful diet, exercise, sufficient sleep, and not abusing the body with drugs or alcohol are ways to help the body to maintain homeostasis.

One of the best defenses the human body has against communicable diseases is the external areas of the body. The skin, nose, and lining of the mouth and throat and eyes help prevent bacteria, viruses, and fungi from invading the body. The human skin is remarkable—when it is exposed to disease-causing agents, it secretes chemicals that can destroy these agents. However, if you examined the human skin under a microscope, you would find harmful microbes there at almost any time. Very few disease-causing organisms can penetrate human skin when it is intact. However, an abrasion or a break in the skin can allow bacteria, viruses, or fungi to enter the body and cause disease.

The eyes, through the use of the tearing action, constantly sweep the disease-causing organisms from their surface. The nose and mouth "catch" the bacteria and viruses—with the hair in the nose or sticky mucus and sweep them out of the areas by action of the cilia. *Cilia* are tiny hairlike projections from cells that, by their sweeping action, move foreign bodies up and out of or away

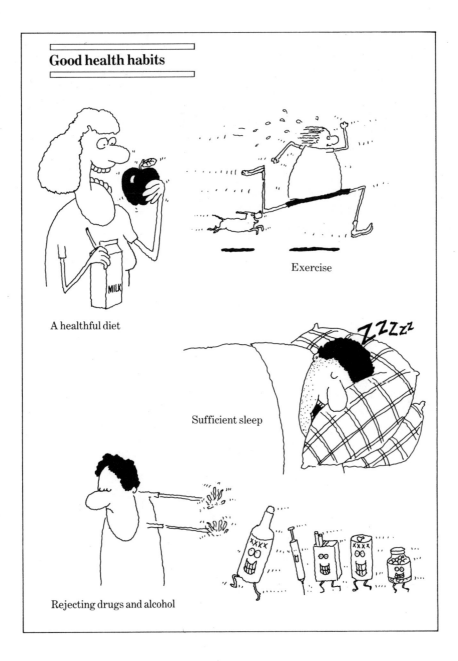

Good health habits

A healthful diet

Exercise

Sufficient sleep

Rejecting drugs and alcohol

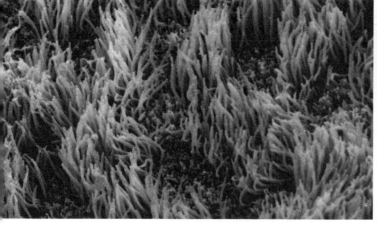

Some of the human body's defenses: (a) scanning electron micrograph (SEM) of cilia, which beat with a wave-like rhythm to propel mucus or fluid across the surface of the cells, lubricating the passages and preventing the accumulation of foreign particles; (b) the tearing action of the eyes which sweeps disease-causing organisms from the surface; (c) the skin, one of the body's first lines of defense

from the body. Coughing and sneezing help to expel disease-causing organisms, too.

The body also has its own microbes on the skin and in the body linings that can destroy other bacteria, viruses, and fungi. Saliva and stomach acids help to destroy invading disease organisms, too.

If, after all of these defenses are brought into play, harmful disease-causing organisms are able to successfully invade the body, it employs other mechanisms of defense to destroy the invaders. These are inflammation, antibody reactions, and the immune reaction.

Remember when you last cut your finger or fell and scraped your knee? If you followed your parent's advice, you washed out the cut or scrape and applied some antiseptic to the damaged area. Those procedures, if you did them carefully and promptly, probably kept you from getting an *inflammation*.

When the area around a cut or abrasion starts to swell and becomes red and painful, we say that the area is inflamed. This is the way that the human body begins to fight the disease-causing organisms that have entered the body through the break in the skin. The swelling in the damaged area shows that there is increased blood flow to the area surrounding the cut. A clear fluid generated by the swollen blood vessels helps to wash away the germs in the area.

Now the antibody reaction takes place: the body sends various white blood cells to the damaged area to destroy the invading germs. The white cells, or corpuscles, which are always present in the blood, find and attack the invading organisms. These cells more or less "eat" the invaders. This process is known as *phagocytosis*. They do this by engulfing the bacteria and then, through a chemical process, dissolving them. (When you have pus in a cut or abrasion, this is what is left of the dead cells of bacteria and the white blood cells.) Once all of this is done, the damaged area begins to regenerate and repair itself.

In the case of communicable diseases, the body uses much the same defenses—that of inflammation, antibody reactions, and the action of the immune system.

Some of the cells that are activated by an invading disease organism even have a memory. For once an infection takes place, some cells retain a memory about the specific infection and remain circulating in the blood for years. If the disease again attacks the individual, these cells, with their memory of previous attacks, stop the infection, giving us immunity to that disease, often for the rest of our lives.

Chapter Four

DIAGNOSIS AND TREATMENT

Bzzzzz! Bzzzzz! Bzzzzz! You reach over to turn off your alarm. As you start to get up, you notice your throat feels a little sore and dry and your nose itches. You get dressed and go downstairs to breakfast. You tell your father you don't want to go to school today because you don't feel well. He feels your forehead and says, "Well, you feel a little feverish; we'd better take your temperature." A few minutes later, he says, "Your temperature is up a little; it's 100°F (38°C). Do you really feel too bad to go to school?"

"No, I guess I'd better go. There's basketball practice, and I really don't feel that bad."

By the time you get home from school that day, your throat feels very sore and raw and it hurts to swallow. You feel hot, and you continually cough and sneeze. As you slump down in a chair, your mother asks how you are feeling and you answer, "Not so good."

She feels your forehead, gets the thermometer, and after a while tells you, "Your temperature is almost 102°F (39°C). Go to bed and I'll bring you some hot soup soon. If you're not better tomorrow morning, we'll take you to the doctor."

The next morning you feel even worse. Your mother calls the doctor and makes an appointment for that afternoon. What the doctor will do is diagnose your illness and then prescribe treatment, as medical practitioners have done for thousands of years.

Almost since the beginning of humans on earth, there has been some sort of diagnosis and treatment of disease by individuals who were given the responsibility by tribes, clans, or kings. Often religious rituals were performed by witch doctors to cure disease, or certain precious stones or special places were thought of as being able to cure disease. The ancient Egyptians even had trained medical doctors who were able to perform operations. However, it was not until Anton van Leeuwenhoek (1632–1723) invented the microscope in the 1600s and actually saw bacteria that we started to see the real causes of disease. And not until the French scientist Louis Pasteur (1822–1895) performed his experiments in 1862 did we begin to understand the relationship between bacteria and disease. Pasteur's work was built on by Robert Koch (1843–1910), a German scientist, who discovered in 1883 that a specific organism was a cause for a specific disease.

Today when an ill person goes to the doctor, the doctor proceeds to discover the cause of the illness—this is called diagnosis—and then prescribes the treatment for the illness. The majority of illnesses that doctors in the United States diagnose are those called upper-respiratory diseases, which include the cold and flu, for which there are no specific cures. Sometimes, diseases are very difficult for the doctor to diagnose because the patient shows no symptoms other than not feeling well. Sometimes the disease masks itself by causing the patient to exhibit symptoms not commonly related to that specific disease.

Some diseases may be diagnosed only through a variety of tests. Blood tests, urine tests, and throat cultures are frequently used. In the case of a culture of the interior of the throat, a sample will be taken, placed in a shallow dish and cultured, or grown. If the patient has a *strep* infection, for example, within a twenty-

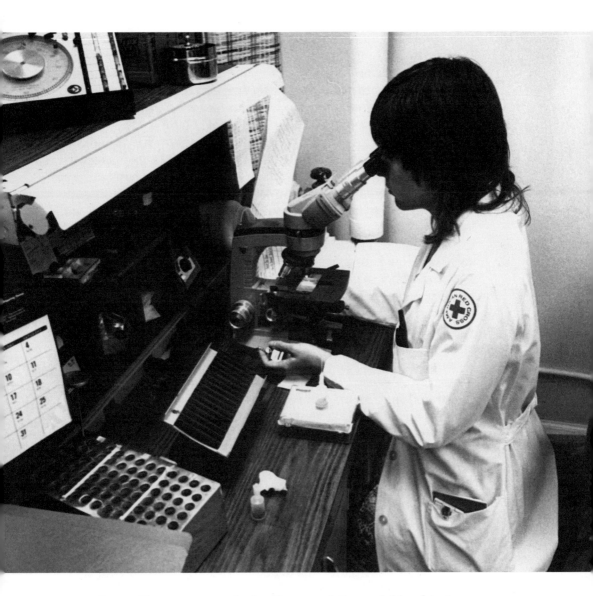

Some diseases can only be diagnosed through blood tests.

four- to forty-eight-hour period the strep bacteria are observable in the culture container and the doctor can then prescribe treatment. Bacteria are classified two ways: gram-positive or gram-negative. These terms come from a specific test made on cultures. If the bacteria, after being dyed, can be seen through a microscope, they are gram-positive. If they don't hold the dye, they can be stained with a dye other than the gram-positive dye to indicate they are gram-negative. Other times the disease is obvious—with chicken pox, the patient is covered with pimplelike spots.

The first person you usually see when visiting the doctor is the doctor's nurse, who will ask about your symptoms, weigh you, and take your temperature. Then the doctor will arrive and will listen to your heart and take your pulse. The doctor will ask you questions such as, How long have you felt ill? Where does it hurt? Do you feel tired? How is your appetite? The doctor will look at your eyes and if you are coughing and sneezing and show symptoms of a bad cold or the flu, will look into your nose, your ears, and, finally, your throat, to see if it is red, discolored, or has spots. Depending upon your symptoms, the doctor then may ask the nurse to take a sample of blood, take a throat culture, and make other tests if necessary. If you are diagnosed as having a bad cold, the treatment prescribed may be only to relieve your symptoms, as there is no cure for a cold. If tests show that you have a strep infection, the treatment would be an antibiotic drug that has the ability to attack and kill the strep bacteria before they do further damage to your body.

IMMUNIZATION

Since the early work of Edward Jenner, Louis Pasteur, and Robert Koch in discovering the causes of communicable diseases, scientists and medical investigators have been constantly searching for ways to prevent these diseases. One area of study is called *immunology*, and the process is called *immunization*. As we saw earlier, the human body has special white cells that remember when a person has caught a particular disease. If the person is exposed later to the same disease, the immune system is alerted to the invading disease-causing organism and protects the person against catching the disease again.

What scientists discovered through their research is that certain diseases may be prevented by immunization. They found that if a person is inoculated (injected) with a small dose of live, attenuated (diluted) disease-causing cells or of dead ones, called *vaccine*, the immune system would be triggered as if the person had caught the disease. Yet, the individual does not actually catch the disease and does not experience the painful symptoms accompanying the disease.

Some diseases have been almost completely stopped because of world- or countrywide immunization programs. A good example of this is the highly contagious and dangerous disease called smallpox, which is now eradicated. Edward Jenner, an English physician, first noticed that people who caught cowpox, a mild disease, never caught smallpox. As a result, Jenner developed a vaccine made from the cowpox virus which gave people immunity from smallpox. Also, in the United States today, the dread disease polio, which can lead to total paralysis or death, has almost disappeared because of immunization. Today, there are vaccines not only for the so-called childhood diseases, but for other diseases, such as the plague, yellow fever, typhus, typhoid fever, and cholera.

The following is the recommended schedule for receiving immunization against childhood diseases:

Immunization	*Age*
Combined diphtheria, tetanus, and pertussis vaccine as well as oral polio vaccine	2 months
Combined diphtheria, tetanus, and pertussis vaccine as well as oral polio vaccine	4 months

*Edward Jenner vaccinates a child against smallpox
using fluid drawn from the hand of Sarah Nelmes,
who had contracted cowpox from milking cows.*

Combined diphtheria, tetanus, and pertussis vaccine	6 months
Rubella, measles, and mumps vaccine	15 months
Combined diphtheria, tetanus, and pertussis vaccine and oral polio vaccine	18 months
Combined diphtheria, tetanus, and pertussis vaccine and oral polio vaccine	5 years

WONDER DRUGS

In the 1930s, the *sulfanomides* (sulfa drugs) were introduced, and penicillin in 1942. They were thought to be drugs that would end the threat of bacteria-caused diseases that often killed their victims. The penicillin family of drugs are made from living organisms, fungi, and then refined in a laboratory. (Penicillin was discovered by Alexander Fleming [1881–1955] in molds growing in a laboratory jar.) Today, many *antibiotics* are made synthetically in laboratories. Other drugs, like the sulfa drugs, were devised from chemical compounds in the laboratory. The drugs were often called "wonder drugs" because at their first applications they seemed capable of curing almost any bacterial disease. However, these drugs and drugs developed later have sometimes caused greater problems than the original disease or infection.

One of the major problems is that they have often been given to patients who are suffering from viral diseases. Antibacterial drugs are unable to cure viral diseases and often cover up the true cause of the disease and sometimes prolong it. For example, patients with influenza (flu), which is caused by a virus, often will demand an antibacterial drug to combat the disease.

Also, there is a continuing increase in the number of severely ill patients whose lives are prolonged by procedures that often suppress or destroy the body's natural immune system. When this happens, the most powerful of the drugs cannot continually destroy disease-causing organisms. For example, many of the treatments prescribed for cancer temporarily or permanently weaken the body's immune system, thus exposing the patient to the risk of catching and dying from pneumonia.

Antimicrobial, or antimicrobic, drugs operate in somewhat the same way as antibiotics. First, when the infection or disease is diagnosed, an appropriate drug is chosen by the doctor. In the case of bacterial infections, the drug prescribed will depend on whether the bacteria are gram-positive or gram-negative. If the patient has streptococcus pneumonia, the appropriate drug is penicillin. Diphtheria would call for the drugs erythromycin or penicillin. A fungal infection, like athlete's foot, would be treated with the antifungal drug griseofulvin.

Antimicrobial drugs are given to patients in one of three ways. (1) The drug may be injected into the body so that it enters the blood system directly. (2) It may be taken orally, that is, swallowed by the patient. In this case the drug is digested in the patient's stomach and then enters the bloodstream. (3) The antimicrobial drug may be applied directly to the infection—such as a skin infection—where it attacks the disease-causing organism directly.

The antimicrobial drug then either affects the functions of the disease-causing organism or its structure. In other words, the antimicrobial drug can inhibit the growth of the disease organism and then allow the body's natural immune system to destroy the organism. Or the drug can actually kill the invading organism by attacking either its coating or interior.

Antibiotics also can be classified as narrow-spectrum or broad-spectrum. Narrow-spectrum antibiotics can treat only specific diseases; broad-spectrum antibiotics can treat a wide range of diseases. Doctors use broad-spectrum antibiotics when they are unsure of which specific bacterium is causing a patient's disease.

Many virus-caused diseases can be prevented through the use of vaccine, such as those for measles, mumps, chicken pox, polio, and even rabies. However, once a viral disease occurs, there are no antibiotic drugs that can destroy the virus and thereby cure the disease. Although there is no cure as yet for viral diseases, they can be treated in a variety of ways. If you catch a cold or the flu, the doctor may prescribe bed rest, drinking a lot of fluids, and aspirin to reduce fever. Other medicines may also be prescribed to help clear up your runny nose, reduce your coughing, or soothe your sore throat. Some viral diseases may be so severe that you have to be hospitalized in order to receive care that only a staff of doctors and nurses and a hospital can supply.

Although antibiotics are ineffective against viral diseases, they are sometimes prescribed if the viral disease is so severe that the body cannot defend itself against possible bacterial infection. That is why when you get a very bad case of the flu your doctor may prescribe a broad-spectrum antibiotic.

Today scientists and doctors are working in laboratories and hospitals around the world to develop antiviral drugs that will work against virus-caused diseases as the sulfa and penicillin drugs work against bacterial diseases. Since 1957, when the substance *interferon* was discovered in human cells, scientists have focused on using it against viral diseases. Interferon is produced by the human cell only when the cell is invaded by a virus. Although interferon does not destroy viruses, it does cause the immune system to become much more active. Also, scientists have isolated another body substance that is produced when the human cells are invaded by viruses, interleukin 1 and 2. However, the broad use of substances like interferon against viral diseases has not been highly successful. Interferon is very expensive and is somewhat unstable, and much more research needs to be done.

Chapter Five

DISEASES YOU CAN CATCH AGAIN AND AGAIN

"Achoo! Achoo!" "If I sneeze again," you think, "I must be catching a cold." Though sneezing twice does not necessarily mean that you are catching a cold, it does mean that some foreign substance is irritating your nose and that's the nose's way of getting rid of dust, virus, or bacteria. But maybe you *are* catching a cold.

THE MOST COMMON COMMUNICABLE DISEASE

The common cold is the communicable disease that causes more time lost from school and work than any other disease. It is the most common communicable disease and can be caught again and again. This is because colds are caused by over one hundred different viruses.

We know that some sections of the population are more likely to catch colds than are others. Children catch more colds than adults; teenage girls get more colds than teenage boys; and women get more colds than men. As you probably already know, people

in the United States get more colds in the winter than in the summer.

Colds are viral infections of the human upper respiratory tract (nose and throat). They are passed from one person to another, usually by airborne droplets that an infected person has either sneezed or coughed into the air. That's why you should always cover your nose or mouth when you sneeze or cough. Also, recent research has shown that you can catch a cold by having your hand contaminated and then touching either your nose or mouth. You are then helping the viruses to travel from the person with a cold to you.

When you catch a cold, you first must be exposed to a cold virus. After a one- to four-day incubation period, you will exhibit the symptoms of a cold. You will start to sneeze and cough and get a stuffy nose. Sometimes you will get either chills or a fever. Often a sore or scratchy throat will develop, too.

After a day or so, the cold will be fully developed. Your nose will run, and you will have to blow it often to get rid of the excess mucus. Your head and throat and upper chest will feel "stuffed-up," too. After about three days, your symptoms will start to go away. However, you may still feel stuffed-up for another week until the symptoms disappear. The cold is communicable to another person for two or three days after you come down with it.

There is no specific way to diagnose a cold. Unlike the procedure for bacterial infections, the doctor will not ordinarily culture the virus because of the length of time needed to perform the test. The doctor usually diagnoses the cold by looking, feeling, and asking questions. At times, though, because you have other symp-

The common cold is the communicable disease that causes more time lost from school and work than any other disease.

toms, such as swollen glands in the neck or highly inflamed or infected tonsils, the doctor may suspect that more than a cold is involved in your illness and order other tests for bacterial infection.

There is no known cure for the cold. The only treatment that can be prescribed is to relieve the symptoms of the cold. For example, the doctor may prescribe aspirin for fever, rest for tiredness, and fluids to help thin the mucous discharges from the nose, to soothe the sore throat, and to replace fluid lost by the body. Sometimes decongestants are prescribed to help dry up the runny and itchy nose.

Some people believe that high doses of vitamin C or sitting under sun lamps can either prevent or cure colds. However, only the substance interferon seems likely to prevent or cure colds. As this substance is so costly, it does not seem feasible at this time. There are many other medicines and preventives that are sold or advertised as "cold cures." It seems that the old advice is best: try to avoid people who have colds, and, if you have one, cover your coughs and sneezes, don't drink out of other people's glasses, and wash your hands often.

FLU VIRUSES

There are several types of influenza, or the flu, as it is commonly known. The flu viruses have the interesting ability to change their character slightly. As a result the body's immune system may not recognize a virus it has previously come in contact with. In other words, if you catch a particular kind of flu this year, next year it may alter itself enough that your immune system will not remember it. As a result, you can catch the flu again, again, and again.

The flu viruses are spread from person to person as a cold is. If you inhale the airborne droplets from the sneezes and coughs of an infected person or touch contaminated objects and then put your hand to your mouth or nose, the flu viruses can invade your body.

Symptoms of flu include chills, high fever, headache, achy body, sore throat, and a runny nose.

There are three types of influenza viruses. Type A, which can often kill people, appears every two to three years, with a new strain every ten years. Type B strikes every four to five years and causes epidemics (the spread of the disease over large areas). And type C, which is uncommon, is usually confined to specific geographic areas.

Influenza can kill people, especially those who are old or suffering from heart, lung, or kidney diseases. In 1918, there was a worldwide flu epidemic that killed over twenty million people. The flu especially strikes school-age children and adults over the age of forty.

Once you have been exposed to an influenza virus, it takes twenty-four to forty-eight hours for the flu symptoms to appear. Once you come down with flu, you often get chills, a high fever, headache and an achy body, sore throat, and a runny nose. These symptoms usually are gone in three to five days. However, a person may feel weak and tired for several more days.

If the fever persists for more than five days, often it indicates that there are complications or that another infection has attacked the body. Many of these complications may be bacterial infections and can be treated with antibiotics. A common complicating disease is pneumonia, which can be very serious if not diagnosed and treated.

Often influenza is misdiagnosed as a bad cold. There is a laboratory method of diagnosing influenza by taking cultures from the nose and throat of the patient. In the case of epidemics, this is important to confirm the type of influenza. Once it is known that there is an influenza epidemic, doctors can diagnose the disease on the basis of observations.

Treatment of flu is much like the treatment for a cold: aspirin for fever, bed rest, lots of liquids, and sometimes over-the-counter drugs for the relief of coughing, sore throat, and runny nose. Because the flu is caused by a virus, antibiotics are not prescribed because they will not be effective. There is an antiviral agent that can be prescribed that may help to reduce the symptoms of the disease. There are vaccines available for influenza, commonly called "flu shots," which are usually effective in around 75 percent of the individuals inoculated. But these are developed from the previous year's virus, and if the virus has mutated (changed), the vaccines will not be effective. To prevent passing the flu virus to others, you should follow the same precautions as with colds.

DIARRHEA

Diarrhea, like the cold and the flu, is a broad term for several different diseases affecting the intestinal tract that are caused by many different organisms. For example, *salmonellosis*, often called food poisoning, is caused by the bacterium *Salmonella* and is usually caused by eating or drinking contaminated water or food, though the disease may come from contact with infected humans or animals. *Shigellosis* is a bacterial infection of the intestinal tract caused by the bacterium *Shigella*. The disease is transmitted directly by the fecal-oral route, contact with contaminated objects, and occasionally the housefly.

Enterobacteriaceae are a group of rod-shaped bacilli (a type of bacteria) that cause a wide variety of intestinal infections. Of this group, the bacterium *Escherichia coli* are thought to be the major cause of diarrheal illness in children in the United States.

Though the bacterium *E. coli* exists naturally in the gastrointestinal tract, infections may be caused by *E. coli* bacteria not naturally found in the tract. The disease is usually transmitted by direct contact with an infected person, through contaminated food or water, or through excessive contact with contaminated articles. When these bacteria invade the intestinal tract, toxins are produced that interact with intestinal juices and cause excessive loss of chloride and water.

The symptoms of *E. coli* infection are abrupt watery diarrhea and stomach pain and cramps. Another form of the disease will cause chills and abdominal cramps, and the stools, or bowel matter, may contain blood and pus.

Because *E. coli* naturally occurs in the gastrointestinal tract, culturing to diagnose the disease is of little value. Diagnosis, then, usually depends on the signs, or symptoms, of the disease, as observed by the doctor and described by the patient. Diagnosis must rule out other diseases with similar symptoms, such as salmonellosis and shigellosis. Treatment for *E. coli* infections consists of isolating the patient to prevent spread of the disease, having the patient drink a lot of fluid to replace those lost in excessive bowel movements, and, in some cases, prescribing antibiotics.

Chapter Six

CHILDHOOD DISEASES

Chicken pox (varicella), German measles (rubella), diphtheria, measles (rubeola), mumps (parotitis), and polio (poliomyelitis) are commonly called childhood diseases. This is because ordinarily if a person is going to catch one of these diseases, he or she will catch it in childhood and, as a result, get immunity from the disease. These diseases can vary in how strongly they affect a person, and sometimes the person will be infected very lightly and suffer very little from the disease. However, even a light case will ordinarily result in immunity from the disease for the rest of the person's life.

CHICKEN POX

Chicken pox is a very contagious virus-caused disease. It is prevalent in early childhood, and having the disease usually, but not always, gives immunity for life. There is a vaccine available for chicken pox, but it is not widely used because there is some doubt about its long-range effect and the need for a vaccine for such a mild disease. It is recommended, though, for children who have

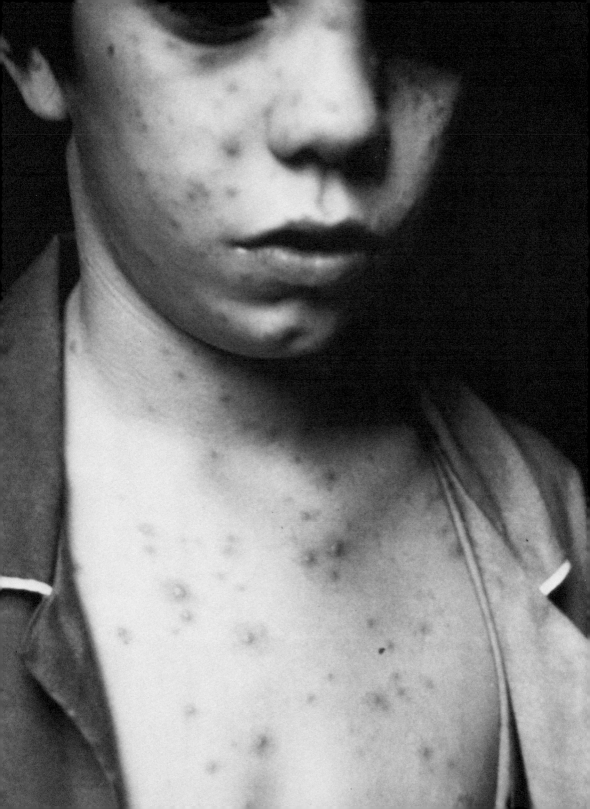

diseases of the immune system, such as leukemia, because in these cases chicken pox can be a fatal disease.

Chicken pox has an incubation period of from two to two and a half weeks after exposure. The disease is passed from one person to another by way of the respiratory tract (mouth, throat, and lungs) in the early stages of the disease. Later in the course of the disease, it may be transmitted by contact with fluids from the rashlike sores on the skin. At first, only a rash appears. The rash later turns into pimplelike bumps, and then into clear-fluid–filled bumps. These clear-fluid–filled bumps become cloudy, break easily, and scab over. Usually, these bumps appear on the body, face, and head. Occasionally, though, they may cover the entire body, including the soles of the feet and inside the mouth. The rash is usually accompanied by a mild fever, loss of appetite, and a tired feeling.

Usually the doctor relies on the appearance of the patient to diagnose the disease. However, chicken pox also can be diagnosed easily through laboratory tests, if needed.

Because chicken pox is so highly contagious, the patient is isolated until most of the clear bumps and scabs disappear. If the pox or skin lesion itches, lotions and soda baths will help bring relief. Antibiotics will not cure the disease, as it is caused by a virus. However, if the patient constantly scratches the rash and bumps, there is danger of a bacterial infection that should be prevented with antibiotics. Sometimes people who have been exposed to a family member with an especially bad case of chicken pox can receive a shot of V. Z. immunoglobulin. This will not prevent them from catching the disease, but will reduce the impact of the disease if they do come down with it.

A boy with chicken pox

GERMAN MEASLES

German measles, or rubella, is a contagious virus-caused disease. No one is quite sure how the word *German* became attached to measles because this disease did not come from Germany, just as chicken pox didn't come from chickens. German measles is found around the world and, from time to time, epidemics of the disease occur.

German measles is transmitted from person to person by contact with discharge from the infected person's nose or sometimes contact with the blood, urine, or stool. After exposure, an incubation period of two to two and a half weeks passes before the onset of the disease. Usually the disease is first noticed when the individual gets a fever and/or headache and sometimes swollen glands in the neck. Red spots start to appear on the face and then move downward to the chest and stomach. Often inflammation of the linings of the nose and eyes will occur.

As German measles is sometimes very mild, some persons will not even know they have the disease. Complications may occur, but they are very rare. A doctor can diagnose the disease easily if the patient has the rash and swollen lymph glands and has recently been exposed to the disease.

Treatment for the disease is rather simple: bed rest if needed, isolation because the disease is so contagious, and fever-reducing or pain-reducing drugs, if needed. German measles is for most people a mild disease. However, for pregnant women it can be a very serious disease. If the mother-to-be becomes infected with German measles in the first three months of her pregnancy, there is a good chance of a spontaneous abortion (the baby will be born before it is mature enough to live or will be born dead). If that doesn't happen and the woman gives birth to a live child, there is a high possibility that the child may suffer from multiple birth disorders. These can include deafness, cataracts (a membrane forms over the eyes), heart disease, and mental retardation. Today, it is thought, too, that congenital German measles (German measles existing in the body at birth) may cause diseases that don't show up until much later in life, such as diabetes. (Diabetes is a disease which causes the body not to be able to use sugar and can lead to death or other diseases if not properly treated.)

There is a live-virus vaccine available for the prevention of German measles and it seems to work quite well. The vaccine is highly recommended for females before they become of child-bearing age. If they have already reached *puberty* (are able to bear children), they should make sure that they don't become pregnant until at least three months after receiving the vaccine. Occasionally, the vaccine may cause a reaction, such as fever or a slight rash or even shock.

MEASLES

Rubeola or morbilli, known simply as measles, is one of the most highly communicable and often the most dangerous of the childhood diseases. There is a vaccine for measles, which, in the United States today, has greatly reduced the number of measles cases. But in underdeveloped countries, measles can be a fatal disease.

Measles is spread from one person to another either by direct contact or from airborne droplets coming from the infected person's mouth or nose. It takes from one and a half to two weeks after the person is exposed for the disease to develop. The first signs of the disease are fever, coughing, runny nose, eye inflammation, and sensitivity to light. After four or five days, small blue spots, surrounded by a red ring appear in the mouth. After four or five more days the spots in the mouth disappear and the fever rises again, sometimes to as high as 105°F (41°C). Then a dull-red rash begins to cover the body, starting behind the ears, proceeding to the forehead and then downward until the whole body is covered. Recovery from the disease begins two or three days after the body is covered with the rash and the fever peaks. Two or three days later, the rash starts to fade and the infected patient can begin activity again.

(49)

Measles is fairly easily diagnosed by a physician, especially from the body-covering rash or the spots in the mouth of the patient. Occasionally it may be misdiagnosed in its early stages, but when the body rash appears, it is easily diagnosed.

Treatment for measles is plenty of bed rest, drinking lots of fluids, and taking aspirin or another kind of fever-reducing medicine. Antibiotics are not helpful because the disease is caused by a virus, and even though the patient does have a cough, cough medicines are not usually prescribed.

Most people recover easily from measles. However, the disease can cause severe complications in some. These are called *secondary infections*. For example, measles may lead to bacterial pneumonia, an infection of the lung which can be treated with antibiotics; otitis media, an inflammation of the middle ear which can lead to deafness if not treated with antibiotics; and encephalitis, an infection of the membranes (the covering) of the brain or spinal cord.

MUMPS

Mumps (parotitis)—a viral disease, like the other childhood diseases—is transmitted from one person to another by way of saliva droplets sprayed into the air or by direct contact. The mumps virus can live over three months at room temperature. The incubation period, once a person is infected, is from two to three and one-half weeks. People who have had mumps once are immunized for the rest of their lives.

Though one-third of the persons who get mumps do not show any symptoms of the disease, the disease can be quite painful for those who develop a full-blown case. Mumps usually begins with

A small child with measles.
Because of the rash, this disease
is usually easy to diagnose.

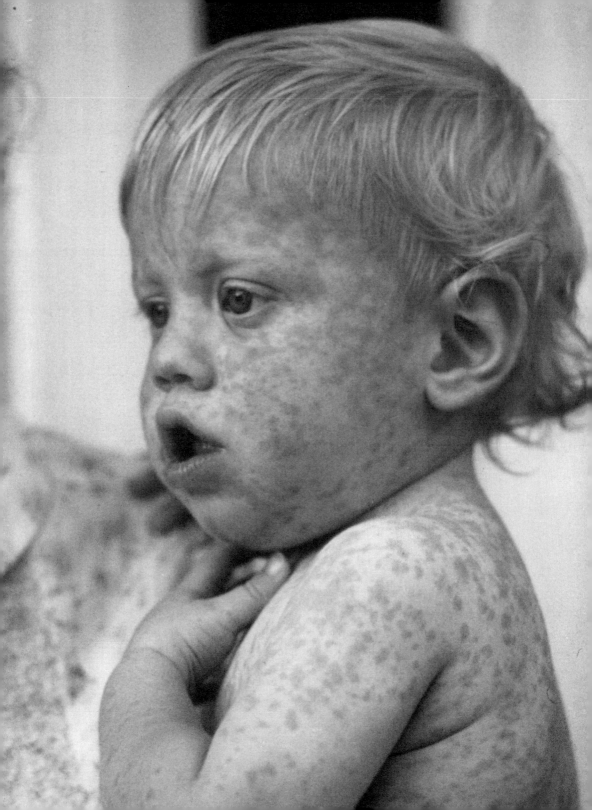

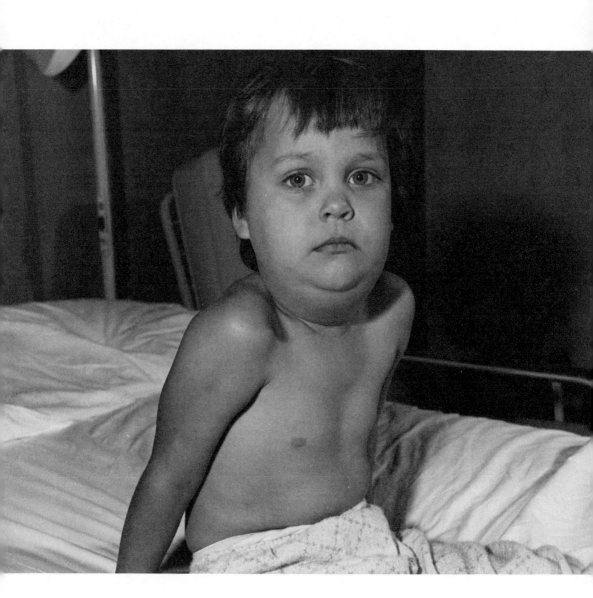

A full-blown case of mumps is hard to mistake.
The swelling around the neck is obvious.

tiredness, lack of appetite, fever, and an earache. Within a day or two, the fever may go up from 101°F (38°C) to 104°F (40°C). At the same time, the parotid gland (a gland just below the ear) will become swollen, and chewing or swallowing will become painful. Sometimes only one side of the jaw is affected, rather than both sides.

For most people, mumps is just a disease to endure. For some young males and older men, however, it can be a more serious disease. For them, the disease may not only affect the glands of the jaw, but move down into the male sexual glands and cause swelling of the glands accompanied by vomiting, fever, chills, and abdominal pains. If this happens, it may cause sterility, the inability to father children, in a very few adults. Mumps may also cause, among other diseases, meningitis, inflammation of the kidneys, inflammation of the heart, and arthritis.

Though laboratory tests can determine the presence of mumps, they are usually not needed. This is because the doctor usually can diagnose the disease by observing the swelling of the neck and determining whether or not the person has been recently exposed to someone else with the disease. Once the diagnosis of mumps has been made, the treatment prescribed is bed rest, drugs for fever and pain, plenty of fluids, avoidance of foods that need lots of chewing, and cold or hot compresses applied to the swollen glands to relieve pain. The patient should be isolated from others because of the highly infectious nature of the disease.

Today in the United States, most children are vaccinated against mumps through the use of diluted live-virus vaccine. In other places in the world that do not have concentrated vaccination programs, there may be, from time to time, epidemics of mumps.

POLIO

Poliomyelitis, better known as polio, was, until the 1950s, one of the most dreaded of the communicable diseases. In the early part of the 1900s, the disease reached epidemic levels throughout the world. Even today, we still see outbreaks of polio in populations that have not been vaccinated against the disease.

Dr. Jonas Salk, in 1955, presented to the world a vaccine for the prevention of polio. The vaccine contained dead viruses which, when injected, caused the human immune system to develop antibodies that prevented the disease. Later, the Sabin vaccine was developed, which is taken by mouth. Today, it is the most commonly used vaccine for preventing the disease. The Sabin vaccine is made up of live but weakened polio viruses.

Polio is transmitted directly from person to person by way of nose and throat secretions and by way of human feces. The incubation period can be from as little as five days to over a month. The virus enters the body, multiplies in the lower intestinal tract, and then spreads to the blood. The disease then takes one of three courses. The first is that the infected person has no real indication that he or she has the disease. The second is that the person seems to be suffering from a cold. The third is that the disease strikes the nervous system and either causes paralysis or a major case of the nonparalytic form. The nonparalytic form causes fever; earache; vomiting; pain in the back, arms, and legs; muscle spasms; and muscle tenderness.

Paralytic polio usually appears five to seven days after the onset of the disease. The symptoms of the disease are stiff neck, loss of reflexes, constipation, urine retention, and swelling of the stomach. If the virus attacks the brain, in addition to paralysis of the limbs, the patient will have difficulty in swallowing, chewing, and breathing. This may lead to shock and death.

Diagnosis, depending on the stage of the disease, can range from the obvious symptoms of paralysis, to laboratory tests. In laboratory tests, cultures taken from the patient's throat and feces are examined under a microscope to isolate the virus.

Because polio is a virus, drug treatment is used only to relieve the pain and fever. Also, hot, moist packs can be applied to the

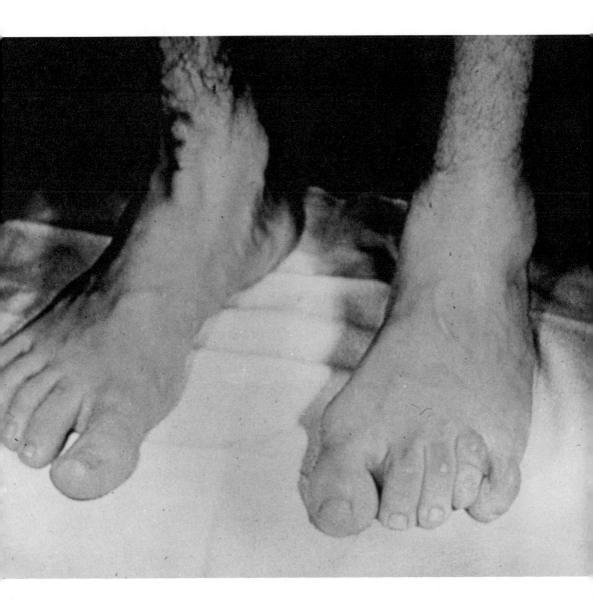

Close-up of both feet of a polio victim

muscles to help relieve the pain. Bed rest, proper food, and fluids are also prescribed. In cases of paralysis, physical therapy is called for to restore the paralyzed limbs and to keep what muscle tone is left. Braces, corrective shoes, and even corrective surgery may also be needed.

Fortunately today, because of the vaccine available, polio is not the dreaded killer and crippler that it once was. However, there are still countries in the world where the disease continues to break out.

DIPHTHERIA

Diphtheria is a highly contagious bacteria-caused disease that usually affects the throat, but may also attack the eyes, ears, and, rarely, the intestinal and urinary tracts. If untreated, it can cause death. Also, diphtheria bacteria may affect the skin and appear in deep cuts or wounds. Fortunately, there is a vaccine for diphtheria, and in the United States and almost everywhere else in the world diphtheria is today a fairly rare disease.

Diphtheria bacteria are passed from one person to another by contact or from sneezes and coughs by persons who show symptoms of the disease as well as by some who show no symptoms but are *carriers*.

The incubation period for diphtheria is about a week. A sore throat, a cough, hoarseness, and runny nose are the first symptoms. However, the major symptom of the disease is the formation of a membrane (a skin or covering) near the tonsils in the throat. What happens is that the tissues of the throat start to ooze a thick fluid, which binds together and forms a membrane, or skin. This membrane can be very dangerous to the infected person. If untreated, it can grow across the airway and completely cut off the person's air supply, causing suffocation and death.

Other complications of the disease can be heart disease, kidney disease, and inflammation of the nervous system. Also, diphtheria may cause pneumonia.

Diagnosis of the disease can be done by taking a throat culture and examining it under a microscope to detect the bacteria. Or, the doctor will see in the throat the membrane that distinguishes this disease from other infections.

Diphtheria can be treated with antibiotic drugs, since it is caused by bacteria. An *antitoxin* may be prescribed, too.

The diphtheria patient should be isolated from other people as the disease is highly contagious. If family members have not received the diphtheria vaccine, they should do so.

It is important to remember that although there have been great advances made in the control of childhood diseases, a great deal more work needs to be done. Since 1978, the World Health Organization (WHO) has been carrying out a worldwide immunization program in an effort to reduce the number of deaths—estimated at 3.5 million annually—from childhood diseases.

Chapter Seven

MEDICAL PROGRESS CAN BE HAZARDOUS TO YOUR HEALTH

When the sulfa drugs were first introduced in the 1930s to combat communicable diseases, they were hailed as "wonder drugs." They were thought to be able to cure many diseases. Since that time, many bacteria have developed resistance to the drugs. This was true, too, in the use of penicillin. Scientists have had to continue to modify the basic penicillin drug and develop new synthetic ones.

In the case of viruses, vaccines have been developed to give people immunity. However, with the possible exception of such substances as interferon, which was discussed earlier, there has not been a discovery of a substance that will stop viral infections. Also, because there are so many different kinds of viruses, it has been difficult to develop drugs that would work against all of them.

People who have viral diseases such as colds or the flu often demand antibiotic drugs from their doctors to cure their disease. As mentioned earlier, antibiotics are effective against bacteria but not viruses, so they cannot cure viral diseases. Taking antibiotics will not help those patients. Worse than that, the antibiotics may actually harm them. An antibiotic often kills harmless or useful bacteria, which are always present in the body, while allowing some harmful bacteria to multiply, flourish, and cause infection.

It is interesting to note, too, that some diseases thought to have been controlled by either immunization programs or drugs are starting to break out again. A case in point is whooping cough (pertussis). This disease, for which a vaccine is generally available, has started to increase in the United States and elsewhere today. The reason is that some people believe that the vaccine often causes side effects. Though those side effects are not as serious as the disease, parents are not having their children immunized. Other diseases sometimes reappear because people don't think they have to worry about them and relax their health practices or because the diseases were never entirely overcome.

Advances in health, medical science, and nutrition have allowed people to live longer. The very fact that we do live longer increases the risk of catching an infection. Our immune system is not as strong when we are older and may allow us to catch diseases for which we have no natural immunity.

Some infections are appearing in people who are treated for other diseases. In organ transplant and cancer cases, powerful drugs are given to the patient either to suppress the immune system to prevent organ rejection or to kill the cancer cells. This is called immunosuppression therapy. As the patient is already weakened from the disease or the operation, the additional suppression of the immune system leaves the patient wide open for an infection or communicable disease. Patients will often catch pneumonia or get an infection at the site of the operation or where tubes or catheters are implanted in the body. Sometimes, they will come down with rare or uncommon diseases. Therefore, patients in this category need to be watched very closely and antibiotics need to be given to them for long periods of time.

Chapter Eight

THE GREAT PLAGUES AND EPIDEMICS

The plague! This is a term that for hundreds of years terrorized humans around the world. "Plague" is used to describe several diseases. There was the black plague, the white plague, and the red plague. Many of the so-called plague diseases were known by other names, too: typhus, syphilis, English sweating disease, and the black death.

The plague as we know it today is the bubonic, or black, plague. This disease is still found occasionally in the western part of the United States. It is not transmitted from person to person, but from rodents (rats and mice) to fleas that live on the rodents and then to humans by the bite of the flea.

The bubonic plague can cause the pneumonic plague, which *is* transmitted from one person to another. This can happen in the last stages of bubonic plague if the plague victim develops pneumonia. The victim will cough up blood and saliva and, through the airborne droplets from the coughs, the bacteria are spread to other people, who may become infected.

The various forms of the plagues have, over the centuries, killed tens of millions of people throughout the world. In Europe,

A fifteenth-century painting of a plague hospital

where better records were kept, historians and physicians noted that whole populations of cities were killed by a disease. Plagues often were more important in determining the outcome of wars than the battles themselves. In fact, a group of diseases were known as "military fevers" because they would strike primarily soldiers and armies. Today, we think that many of these "fevers" were the diseases we know as measles, chicken pox, and scarlet fever.

As the European countries invaded and conquered the Americas, plague and other diseases played an important part in conquering the natives. *Epidemics* are diseases that are not confined to any particular groups of people, but will affect large areas or populations. The native Indians in Mexico and North America had not been exposed to many European diseases and therefore had no immunity to them. It is said that one sailor from a Spanish ship brought smallpox to Mexico and caused the death of over three million native Indians. The powerful native tribes were then so weakened by the plagues that the Spaniards had an easy time conquering them. The Indians of North America suffered the same fate. The English, French, and Spaniards brought diseases with them that caused a great many deaths among the natives and made it much easier for the Europeans to conquer them.

Many of the plague diseases that historians described seem not to exist today. Also, as the plague diseases continually infected populations, the people who survived the disease often had immunity, and each continuing wave of infection got weaker and weaker. Others, like smallpox, were destroyed by medical advancement: the invention of vaccines and the development of antibiotic drugs. For example, cases of the bubonic and the pneumonic plague today can be fatal to up to 60 percent of the patients without treatment. For those who are treated with antibiotic drugs, death occurs only in around 18 percent.

Chapter Nine

DEADLY COMMUNICABLE DISEASES

Many diseases kill. Some of these killing diseases are inherited, and some are the result of our abusing our body until we come down with them. A third group of killer diseases are the communicable diseases, which are usually passed from one person to another like the common cold. Some of these diseases were once so contagious that they swept across countries and regions, killing hundreds of thousands. Fortunately, many communicable diseases now have been almost wiped out due to vaccine programs and antibiotics. Others wait until we are run-down from other diseases and then strike, while still others, though unknown today, sit and wait in out-of-the-way places in the world ready to strike again.

PNEUMONIA

Of the deadly communicable diseases, pneumonia is one of the most common, and bacterial pneumonia is the fifth leading cause of death in patients who have been suffering from other diseases or who are old. Pneumonia can be caused by viruses, bacteria, and fungi, as well as other disease-causing organisms. Also, pneumonia may be caused by the inhalation of fumes of dangerous chemicals, as well as by the vomiting of food and stomach acids, the residues of which are then inhaled into the lungs, resulting in bacterial pneumonia.

Pneumonia can be caught by inhaling viruses and bacteria present in the air or fungi stirred up by wind or can result from viruses or bacteria already present in the human body. Pneumonia often develops in patients being treated for cancer because they are being treated by very strong drugs. In their action of killing cancer cells, those drugs also greatly weaken the body's immune system, allowing bacterial or viral pneumonia to easily develop.

The symptoms of the disease in its early stages can often be confused with a bad cold or influenza. In fact, secondary pneumonia following influenza is a very deadly type of pneumonia. In pneumonia the early symptoms are coughing, chest pain, fever, and chills that cause the patient to shake.

The physician diagnoses pneumonia using several different tools. Besides the signs that the doctor can see and hear, for example, noises (called rales) in the lungs, an X ray of the chest is the best diagnostic tool to discover whether the patient has pneumonia. The X-ray picture of a pneumonia victim will show the lungs clogged with mucus. Laboratory tests of lung secretions and blood will also indicate whether the patient has pneumonia or not. Another test is to tap the lung by inserting a needle through the wall of the chest and draining fluid from the pleural cavity, the area surrounding the lungs, for analysis.

Depending on the cause of pneumonia, the treatment will vary. If the disease is caused by bacteria, an antibiotic drug like penicillin is administered. In the case of viral pneumonia, antibiotic drugs will not be effective, and only a drug called amantadine will work on type A influenza pneumonia. Other drugs are available for pneumonia caused by organisms other than bacteria and viruses. Other treatment for pneumonia is bed rest, adequate fluids, and nutrition. In some cases, oxygen therapy will be needed so that the patient

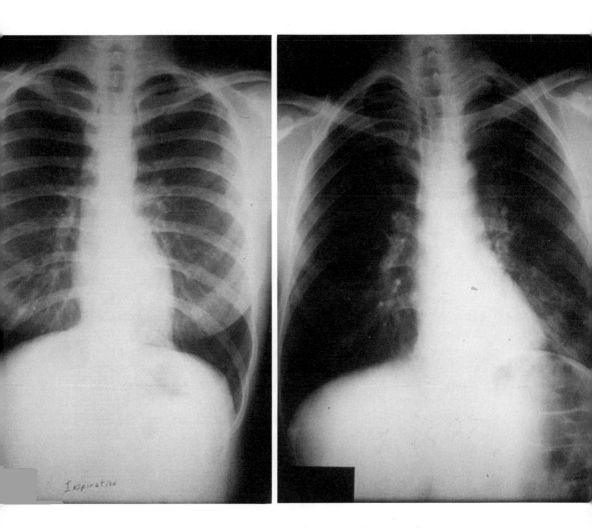

On the left, an X ray of a normal chest; on the right a chest X ray of a patient with pneumonia

can breathe more easily and get an adequate amount of oxygen into the blood system.

The patient, whether at home or in the hospital, should cough into a disposable bag in order to prevent the spread of the disease. Often, fluids from the lungs will have to be sucked out and the patient should understand why and how the procedure is done. The patient should cough a lot and do deep-breathing exercises to help clear the lungs.

People can prevent pneumonia of certain types by getting vaccinated for influenza and not taking antibiotic drugs for minor virus-caused infections. Receiving antibiotic drugs too often may make an individual more susceptible to antibiotic-resistant organisms.

MENINGOCOCCAL INFECTIONS

"Meningococcal infections" refers to several diseases that affect the nervous system, especially the brain and spinal cord. One of these infections is highly contagious and will break out from time to time in army camps filled with new recruits. The disease is passed from person to person by way of airborne droplets discharged from the nose and mouth. This is the disease that has caused great epidemics. Its victims were often covered with a rash or spots and, in days before scientific diagnosis, the disease was confused with other diseases. In its last stages, if not treated, the disease will lead to death in six to twenty-four hours.

MENINGITIS

Meningitis is a specific disease that attacks the membranes of the brain and spinal cord. Usually meningitis results from an infection moving from one site to another. For example, the same disease organism may cause influenza, which then causes pneumonia, which then causes meningitis. The symptoms of bacterial meningitis are much like other bacterial infections: body weakness, severe headache, fever and chills, stiff neck, and vomiting. Also, the patient's eyes may become light-sensitive and the patient will have such extreme spasms that the back will arch so much that the body will rest on the heels and the head.

Diagnosis of the disease can be done from symptoms that the doctor can see, like the arched back. The surest test is to extract fluid from the spine and take cultures from the nose and throat for laboratory analysis. Treatment for bacterial meningitis is antibiotics. Other drugs may be given to control the heartbeat as well as to reduce fever. Bed rest, adequate food and fluids, and isolation from others are also prescribed.

Since the disease may cause convulsions and behavior change, the patient should be watched closely. If the patient's fever shoots up unexpectedly, it may be a sign of heart failure. The patient will also exhibit memory loss for a period of time.

If meningitis is treated promptly, recovery rates, with little side effects, are excellent. If no treatment is received, 70 to 100 percent of those infected will die. Infants and elderly persons do not recover as well and are more likely to die, even if treated. There is no specific treatment for viral meningitis except for supportive treatment such as bed rest and proper nutrition.

HEPATITIS

Hepatitis is a virus-caused disease. It wasn't until the 1970s, with the advancement of the electron microscope, that the viruses causing this disease were fully observed. The disease in its later stages is easily discernible because the patient becomes jaundiced. The patient's skin and even eyes take on a distinct yellow color. There are three types of viral hepatitis: type A (infectious), type B (serum), and type non-A, non-B.

Type A hepatitis is an extremely infectious disease more common among children. The disease is transmitted in a number of ways, but usually by human feces entering the mouth. That is, people often get type A by eating contaminated food, especially seafood that has come in contact with sewage. Type B hepatitis is usually transmitted by way of infected blood transfusions or serum, but also can be caught by contact with human secretions. There are over seventy thousand cases of hepatitis in the United States every year. The disease is common among drug addicts because they often share contaminated needles to inject drugs. Among homosexuals, the number of cases of the disease is increasing because of oral and anal sexual contact.

The symptoms of the various types of hepatitis are somewhat similar. The incubation period for type A is between two and six weeks, while type B may take anywhere from six to twenty-six weeks. The onset of type A is very quick, but type B develops much more slowly. The onset of type B hepatitis is headache, runny nose, cough, tiredness, lack of appetite, sensitivity of the eyes to light, and fever. The patient may also lose the senses of taste and smell.

Hepatitis primarily attacks the liver. The liver is the largest of the internal organs and performs several vital functions. It detoxifies harmful substances, stores vitamins, secretes bile, and metabolizes (turns into energy) carbohydrates, fats, and proteins. Because of the importance of the liver to good functioning of the human body, when the liver is attacked by the hepatitis virus, the body suffers a great deal. Not only does the liver become enlarged and painful, but its operation starts to shut down. One of the obvious indications is when the skin becomes jaundiced. Full recovery from hepatitis may take up to six months.

Jaundice is one of the more obvious signs of hepatitis. But to help confirm the diagnosis, doctors ask patients about their exposure to chemicals, their food intake, and whether they have had recent blood transfusions or injections, have had their ears pierced, or have been around anyone with the disease. Laboratory tests of a patient's blood or a liver *biopsy* (removal of a small piece of the liver by a needle from the outside of the abdomen) will determine if the patient has hepatitis.

As the various types of hepatitis are caused by viruses, there is no specific treatment. However, if type A is caught early in the course of the disease, or if the person is known to have been exposed, gamma globulin will be prescribed and it will be highly effective in fighting the disease if given within two weeks of exposure. Gamma globulin can also be used to combat type B, but it is not quite as effective as against type A. There is also a newly developed vaccine for type B which is effective.

Other treatment prescribed is bed rest, isolation, and taking care to prevent transmitting the disease to others. Because hepatitis patients have little or no appetite, meals should be small and high in protein and calories. In extreme cases, steroids are prescribed to give the patient a sense of well-being and improve the appetite.

Those infected with type A hepatitis usually recover well. For those with type B, recovery may not be as good and type B hits the elderly much harder. About 25 percent of those with type B hepatitis whose disease progresses will die from liver failure.

ORGAN AND SECONDARY INFECTIONS

As we have seen, many communicable diseases directly affect certain organs of the body. Others will affect organs of the body as an indirect result of the disease. The bacteria staphylococcus and streptococcus, for example, cause a number of diseases, ranging from pneumonia and scarlet fever to Saint Vitus's dance and skin infections. At the same time they are causing the disease, these bacteria may also attack other organs. A streptococcus infection of the throat may turn into rheumatic fever and cause heart damage. A sinus infection may turn into meningitis or cause brain abcesses, pus-filled pockets in the brain. A simple bladder infection may invade the kidneys and cause nephritis. Mumps may cause inflammation of the pancreas.

Viruses also attack organs directly. It is thought that a virus causes intussusception, a disease that causes a collapsing of the bowel (intestine). The disease is fatal if not treated, usually by surgery, within twenty-four hours. Influenza viruses may affect the heart, lungs, brain, and other organs. German measles may cause birth defects. Chicken pox may cause pneumonia, heart infection, liver disease, and even arthritis, a disease of the joints. Valley fever, a disease caused by a fungus, may spread to the rest of the body and cause abcesses and can be fatal up to 60 percent of the time. It is apparent, then, that no part of the body is safe from communicable disease caused by bacteria, viruses, fungi, and parasites.

Chapter Ten

SEXUALLY TRANSMITTED DISEASES

There are a number of communicable diseases that are sexually transmitted. The disease that is receiving the most publicity lately is the dangerous disease AIDS. However, there are a number of other sexually transmitted diseases that are quite common around the world, can cause death, and have been with us a long time.

These diseases are usually caused by sexual intercourse between males and females or sometimes between persons of the same sex. Occasionally these diseases can be transmitted in other ways—drug users using dirty needles, mothers transmitting the disease to their unborn children, and, rarely, through infected articles such as toothbrushes or other personal articles.

SYPHILIS

Of these sexually transmitted diseases, the one that has the longest history is syphilis. There seems to be some argument as to whether syphilis was brought back to Europe by the sailors of Christopher Columbus's voyages or was already present in Europe. There are passages in the Bible that some feel show syphilis was present in biblical times. It is thought that some Roman emperors who seemed to act crazy were in the third stage of syphilis. Henry VIII, king of England, was said to be infected.

Syphilis is caused by a spirochete, a type of bacterium. The disease can be transmitted from the infected person to another almost at any of its three stages. The primary stage lasts from two to four weeks after infection. The first stage of the disease is marked by the appearance of a *chancre*, a raw and open sore, in the genital (sex organ) area. The sore disappears after ten to fourteen days. The second stage develops two to four weeks after the end of the first stage. The victim will develop a fever, a rash that can cover the body, and a sore throat, sometimes accompanied by weight loss and vomiting. The disease can then seem to disappear for several years. The third stage of the disease becomes evident anywhere between three to five years after the victim is infected. The disease at this stage can cause damage to the heart, muscles, and bones, and finally damage the brain—often causing very drastic personality changes—then death.

Syphilis can easily be identified using laboratory tests of the blood. Treatment today is with massive doses of antibiotics, usually penicillin. Before the discovery of penicillin, syphilis was often treated with mercury, bismuth, and arsenic, which are toxic chemicals, and often the cure was worse than the disease. Even today the patient must go back to the doctor frequently to see how the treatment is progressing.

Women who have syphilis can transmit it to their unborn children. Around fifty percent of unborn children with syphilis die at

A scientist examines an electron-micrograph of a spirochete, a type of bacterium that causes syphilis.

birth. Those who do live may have defects or damage to their body that cannot be reversed by medical treatment.

Syphilis is a serious disease and should not be taken lightly. Those who are infected should seek treatment, tell their sexual partners, and report the disease to health authorities.

GONORRHEA

Gonorrhea, a bacterial disease, is the most common of the sexually transmitted diseases. It seems to have been a disease of humans almost since their beginning. An ancient Egyptian document, dated around 3500 B.C., describes the treatment of that day for the disease. Today, in the United States, over three million new cases of the disease are reported every year. It is most common among young adults between the ages of nineteen and twenty-five.

After a person is infected, the symptoms of the disease appear in a few days to a week. Males infected with the disease may not show any signs of the disease at all though. If they do, it may show itself as an inflammation of the urine-carrying tube from the kidney to the bladder or as puslike discharge from the penis. Most females with gonorrhea will not show any symptoms either, but also may have a puslike discharge in the urine, itching and redness of the female glands, and pain in the lower abdomen.

The disease is caused by a bacterium and can be diagnosed in laboratories by taking a sample of the infected area and growing it in a culture. Treatment for gonorrhea was originally the chemotherapeutic agent sulfa and more recently has been penicillin. However, gonorrhea has become resistant to sulfa and is becoming more resistant to penicillin drugs. As a result, the doctor must closely watch the patient to see if the drugs are working as intended. Another complication of the disease is that it may cause eye infection if those who are infected touch their eyes with infected hands. Newborn children may have gonorrhea infection of the eyes if the mother has the disease. These infections must be treated promptly, as the eye infection can be quite severe.

If treated properly and quickly, gonorrhea can be easily cured. If not, the disease can cause women to become sterile, not able to have children. With gonorrhea, unlike many other diseases, a cured person does not become immune and can catch the disease again. There are a growing number of cases of the disease, and it has caused some concern among scientists and doctors because of the increasing resistance of the bacteria to drugs.

HERPES

Another disease that has received wide publicity in recent years is genital, or venereal, herpes. It is a very common virus-caused disease, and the number of cases is increasing. The disease is usually transmitted from one person to another by direct sexual contact. However, it seems that genital herpes may also be transmitted to a person from articles that are infected.

Once the person has been infected, it usually takes from a few days to a week for small fluid-filled sacs to appear on the skin of the sex organs. At first the sacs are painless, but they then break and cause open sores which are quite painful. The infected person may also suffer from fever, tiredness, and painful urination. Doctors diagnose the disease from observation of the sores and by laboratory tests, if needed, of the fluid in the sacs.

The disease is hard to treat because it is virus-caused. Antibiotics may be necessary if a bacterial infection results from the open sores. Some medicated creams may be useful in easing the itch and pain of the sores. Some patients require bed rest. A recently developed antiviral drug does hold some hope in preventing the virus from multiplying.

When the sores are present, the disease is very communicable. For pregnant women who have genital herpes, there is a real threat to their unborn child. For if the child is delivered through the birth canal and the mother's disease is in its active stage, the infant will be infected with the herpes virus. Herpes in newborn children can be a very dangerous disease with a high risk of death. Therefore, it is recommended that pregnant women with active herpes deliver their child by cesarean section, that is, the baby is delivered through an incision cut into the mother's abdomen.

AIDS

AIDS, or acquired immune deficiency syndrome, is one of the most terrifying and dreaded diseases of humans today. It is almost impossible to read a newspaper or magazine without seeing something written about the disease, which not so long ago was not even known to exist. There is a great deal of confusion about the disease in scientists' minds and the number of cases of the disease is increasing daily. There also seems to be increasing evidence that the disease is directly linked to some other diseases that are a threat to public health, for example, the rising number of cases of tuberculosis in AIDS patients.

AIDS is caused by the virus called in this country HTLV-III (human T-cell lymphotropic virus—type III). In Europe the virus is called LAV (lymphadenopathy-associated virus). A milder version of the disease is called ARC, which stands for AIDS-related complex. Of those people who have ARC, only a small portion of them develop AIDS each year. Some individuals show no symptoms of AIDS or ARC, but are infected with the disease. The infection shows up when they are given a blood test for AIDS and the blood shows that the antibody for AIDS is present. Though these people do not presently have the symptoms of the disease, they are considered to be carriers of AIDS and can infect other people.

It is thought today that AIDS originated in Africa. Some scientists believe that the virus causing the disease originated in the African green monkey. The disease is now quite widespread in

Africa and has also spread to Europe and the United States. In 1986, some twenty-one thousand Americans had the disease, while some one hundred thousand to two hundred thousand others were classified as having ARC and another one to two million were thought to have AIDS antibodies in their blood.

AIDS is transmitted from one person to another in several ways. It is a sexually transmitted disease in the majority of cases, especially when body fluids are exchanged. It may also be transmitted by drug users using contaminated needles to inject drugs. A third group of victims are those who have become infected by receiving transfusions of blood containing the AIDS virus. The disease may also be transmitted to an unborn child by an infected mother. At first AIDS was thought to strike only homosexuals and drug users. However, it is now known that it can be transmitted sexually between men and women.

The early signs of ARC and AIDS are often confused with a bad cold or influenza. The early symptoms are excessive tiredness; fever and night sweats; weight loss; enlargement of the glands in the neck, armpits, and groin; a sore throat and cough; unexplained bruising and bleeding; and in some, purple blotches in the skin, which indicate a form of cancer called Kaposi's sarcoma.

If AIDS does develop, the victim may then have a variety of symptoms and a variety of infections and a fast-moving cancer, Kaposi's sarcoma, because the immune system is not working. Victims may also suffer from mental disorders, paralysis, and pain in the legs so bad that they can't bear to be moved.

A search for a cure and an effective treatment for AIDS is now going on in laboratories and hospitals around the world. Scientists are trying various approaches, from developing a vaccine against the disease using smallpox virus as the base, to developing new drugs to kill the virus once a person has become infected. The actor Rock Hudson flew to Europe to be treated by an experimental drug in an attempt to cure his AIDS. However, the drug was unable to save his life.

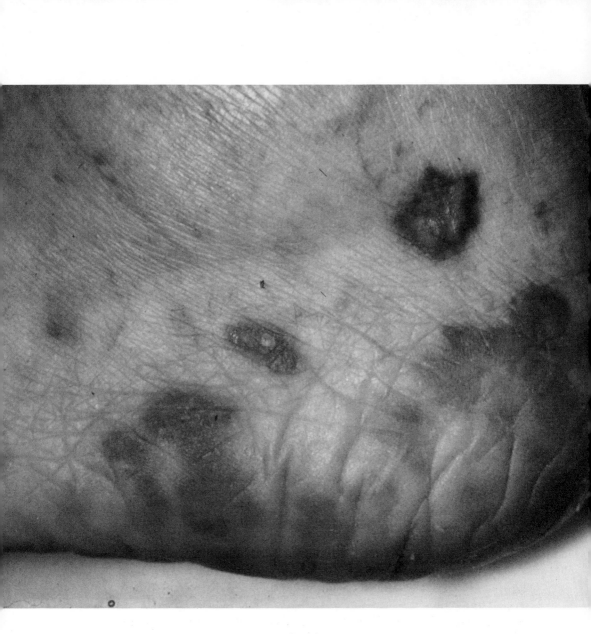

*Kaposi's sarcoma, an opportunistic disease
often found in those who have AIDS,
is marked by purple blotches in the skin.*

Recently, a new drug, AZT, was introduced. The drug does not cure AIDS, but it appears to prolong the lives of AIDS patients by stopping the multiplying of the AIDS virus. The drug is very powerful, however, and does cause some serious side effects.

It is clear that AIDS and ARC are much more widespread than previously thought. Though a weak solution of household bleach and water can easily kill the virus itself if it is on an object or surface, once it gains a hold in the human body it can cause a terrible and fatal disease. We need to know much more about AIDS and other virus-caused diseases. However, it may be some time before these diseases and their causes are fully understood.

Chapter Eleven

IS IT CATCHING?

Have you ever had a wart? If you have, you have had a viral infection of the skin that caused a small tumor, or abnormal growth of cells. Warts are transmitted from one person to another and sometimes—by scratching—from one part of the body to another. At this time, warts are the only known virus-caused tumor, but scientists firmly believe that viruses may cause other abnormal growths as well.

Warts are easily diagnosed by a physician. They come in various shapes, sizes, and colors. Some are flat; others are rough and stick out from the skin. They may occur in groups or alone. They may range in color from pink to dark gray. Some warts just disappear eventually; others have to be removed by a doctor.

Warts can be removed in a number of ways. The doctor may use an electric needle to burn the wart off, or apply liquid nitrogen and freeze it off. Or the doctor may prescribe an acid-based solution to be applied to the wart for a few weeks until it falls off. To remove plantar warts—warts on the soles of the feet—surgery may be required.

As far back as 1908, it was discovered that viruses cause tumors and cancers in animals. Do they affect humans in the same way? There has been a recent surge of research trying to figure out the answer to this question. It is well known, for example, that those people who have had hepatitis B run a much higher risk of getting liver cancer than those who have not had the disease. Right now there is a large experiment being carried on in Taiwan. A great number of people are being vaccinated with the hepatitis B vaccine to see if the program will reduce, in the long run, the number of liver cancers there.

Some scientists believe that viruses alone do not cause cancer. They believe that cancer may be caused by a number of factors along with viruses, such as smoking, stress, heredity, sunlight, exposure to toxic chemicals, and even diet. However, other scientists believe that viruses do indeed directly cause a number of kinds of cancer. Two recent discoveries seem to show that cancer can be caused directly by viruses.

The first discovery came when an outbreak of a rare but fatal form of leukemia occurred on the Japanese island of Kyushu. American scientists examined a few patients with the disease and isolated a virus named HTLV-I in the patients' blood. Scientists have been able to grow this virus in a culture and show that the virus can turn normal cells into cancerous ones. Presently, an experimental vaccine is being worked on and being used with animals to see if it will prevent the disease.

Another virus that scientists suspect causes cancer is the Epstein-Barr virus, a member of the herpes family of viruses that cause a disease called infectious mononucleosis, or the "kissing disease." This disease is quite common in young adults and its symptoms are much like a very bad case of the flu. Some scientists believe that the virus also causes cancer of the nose and throat.

Another virus, which causes warts, is thought by some scientists to cause cervical cancer in women. The cervix is part of the female reproductive system. These HPVs (human papilloma viruses) cannot be grown in culture and therefore are very difficult for scientists to examine more closely.

Along with the above four viruses, which are suspected to cause cancer, scientists and doctors are also investigating another so-called slow virus that is known to cause other diseases. This organism is called a *prion*. Prions are smaller than viruses and are made up of protein; they do not seem to have any genetic material. These slow viruses, or prions, are believed to act much like the suspected cancer-causing viruses. That is, they first cause an infection and many years later the disease. In some people, it may take up to forty years for the original infection to develop into the disease. Scientists are not sure whether these prions are communicable, but some of the evidence suggests that they are.

Kuru is one of the prion-caused diseases. It is found among the headhunting tribes of New Guinea. Symptoms of the disease are tremors, jerking of the limbs, tissue loss, inability to walk or stand, and, finally, death nine to twelve months after the onset of the disease. There is presently a great debate among scientists as to the cause of the disease. At first, it was thought the tribesmen became infected with the disease because they practiced cannibalism, eating the flesh and brains of those they killed in war. Some scientists now say this is not true and that kuru is transmitted through the tribe's women because they handle all of the details of burying the dead. Regardless of how it is transmitted, the disease does take a long time to develop.

The other prion-caused disease is Creutzfeldt-Jakob disease. This disease attacks the brain and causes jerking, tremors, and madness. It, too, usually kills the patient in a year. As with kuru, scientists are unsure how this disease is transmitted and how and why it can bypass the body's immune system and destroy the brain. They are also unsure how the prions multiply and whether they may cause other diseases, too.

Chapter Twelve

THE FUTURE

Most of us are aware of communicable diseases only when we catch a cold or the flu. Luckily most of us recover and go on with our daily lives. Yet many of our ancestors were not so lucky. They died in great numbers and often at early ages from a variety of illnesses. Diseases like smallpox, diphtheria, and communicable plagues killed millions of our ancestors, often in a short period of time.

Today with the discovery of the causes of many communicable diseases and the development of vaccines, some of these dread diseases, like polio, are almost unknown to us. One of the greatest killers, smallpox, has been officially declared to have been wiped out. Yet even today, previously unknown communicable diseases like AIDS are becoming of real concern to individuals, scientists, and governments.

Even though great progress has been made in conquering communicable diseases, scientists have been unable to conquer the common cold, and influenza viruses keep changing to fool our immune systems. Scientists also continue discovering new causes of disease like prions and investigating the possibility that certain mental illnesses may be caused by viruses.

All of this research on disease is costly, both in time and money. Laboratories, hospitals, and research institutions require very expensive equipment and personnel to do the research. At the same time, if the common cold and influenza could be conquered, there would be more than enough saved to further support medical research. Every year around three hundred million cases of colds, flu, and infectious diseases occur in the United States. Health care costs in the United States are now over four hundred billion dollars a year, and this does not cover the costs of lost time at work and school.

There is now scientific work going on that some people believe may lead to the conquering of most communicable diseases in our lifetime. Scientists have been making remarkable progress in developing new drugs and in changing harmful bacteria and viruses through the use of genetic engineering. The genetic engineer can change, substitute, or delete certain genes in a bacterium or virus and cause it to change the way it behaves or acts. In doing so, the "new" bacterium or virus may be used like a vaccine so that people can be protected from the disease by an injection of the genetically altered bacterium or virus.

There is a great deal of optimism about the future of genetic engineering and how it may be able to soon cure bacterial and viral diseases. It may happen someday that diseases from the common cold to cancer will be prevented and we will all be able to lead a life without the threat of communicable disease.

Glossary

Airborne transmission: Transmission of diseases through contaminated saliva droplets or contaminated dust particles that are inhaled. Pulmonary tuberculosis is transmitted this way.

Antibiotics: A chemical substance that has the ability to inhibit or destroy bacteria and other harmful microorganisms.

Antimicrobial: A broad term describing drugs and substances to treat diseases ranging from bacterially- or virus-caused diseases to fungal infections.

Antitoxin: A substance used to counteract a toxin, the poisonous substances generated by a disease.

Bacteria: Small one-cell organisms. They have all the machinery necessary to sustain life and reproduce themselves.

Biopsy: The removal by cutting of a piece of tissue from the body for medical examination.

Carriers: Individuals who have disease-causing organisms and can infect others, yet do not contract the disease themselves.

Cilia: Hairlike projections from the surface of certain cells that sweep back and forth to propel material across the cell surface.

Common vehicle diseases: Diseases that are transmitted by infected food or water, such as salmonella infections.

Contact spread diseases: Diseases that are transmitted by direct person-to-person contact, such as a sexually transmitted disease, or by contact with an infected inanimate object, such as a drinking glass.

Endemic: Refers to a disease that is confined to a particular locality or place or to a particular group of people.

Epidemic: A disease that affects a large number of persons, spreading rapidly from individual to individual.

Escherichia coli (E. coli): The gram-negative bacterium that causes intestinal infections whose symptoms are abrupt, watery diarrhea, cramps, and abdominal pains.

Fungi: Single-cell organisms with rigid cell walls like plant cells but without the green matter. Fungi occur as yeasts or molds.

Homeostasis: The physical and chemical processes that the body uses to maintain a stable internal environment.

Immunization: A process, such as inoculation, that gives a person protection from certain diseases.

Immunology: The study of how the body recognizes materials as harmful or foreign and how the body either neutralizes or eliminates them.

Inflammation: The body's response to an injury indicated by swelling, redness, and pain of the injured area due to increased blood flow to the area.

Phagocytosis: The process by which white corpuscles engulf invading organisms like bacteria in order to destroy them through a chemical process.

Prions: Thought to be disease-causing organisms for several so-called slow virus diseases. Prions are smaller than viruses and consist only of protein.

Rickettsiae: Small, gram negative, bacterialike organisms that cause infections. Like viruses, they need a host cell in order to multiply.

Salmonella: The gram-negative bacterium that causes salmonellosis.

Salmonellosis: One of the most common infections in the United States, it is often called food poisoning. The disease causes fever, diarrhea, abdominal pain, and nausea.

Secondary infection: An infection or disease that follows an initial or first infection or disease. For example, pneumonia often follows the flu because the individual is weakened by flu, allowing the second infection, pneumonia.

Shigella: A gram-negative bacterium that causes shigellosis.

Shigellosis: An acute intestine infection caused by the bacterium shigella, causing fever, vomiting, diarrhea, and pain. Often known as bacillary dysentery.

Strep: An abbreviated term for *streptococcus,* a gram-positive bacterium.

Sulfanomides: A group of chemical compounds that have the ability to inhibit or destroy certain harmful bacteria.

Vaccine: The modified part of a disease-causing microorganism used in an inoculation to prevent that disease.

Vector-borne diseases: Diseases that are transmitted by an intermediate carrier such as a fly or mosquito.

Viruses: Very small organisms visible only through an electron microscope. Viruses cannot reproduce except when in a host cell; they make use of the host cell's biochemical apparatus to reproduce.

For Further Reading

Archer, Jules. *Epidemic!* New York: Harcourt Brace Jovanovich, 1977.

Dekruif, Paul. *Microbe Hunters.* New York: Harcourt Brace and Company, 1966.

Fekete, June, and Peter Ward. *Disease and Medicine.* Maryknoll, N.Y.: Orbis Books, 1985.

Jacobs, Francine. *Breakthrough: The True Story of Penicillin.* New York: Dodd, Mead, 1985.

Nourse, Alan E. *Herpes.* New York: Franklin Watts, 1985.

——— *Viruses.* New York: Franklin Watts, 1983.

——— *Your Immune System.* New York: Franklin Watts, 1983.

Index